PUBLISH IT
SHARING YOUR WRITING ONLINE

Gillian Gosman

PowerKiDS
press.

New York

Published in 2015 by The Rosen Publishing Group, Inc.
29 East 21st Street, New York, NY 10010

First Edition

Editor: Caitie McAneney
Book Design: Mickey Harmon

Photo Credits: Cover (class), pp. 14, 15 Tyler Olsen/Shutterstock.com; cover (background) Attitude/ Shutterstock.com; pp. 3–12, 14–16, 18–20, 22–32 (dot backgrounds) vlastas/Shutterstock.com; pp. 5, 25 michaeljung/Shutterstock.com; p. 7 Monkey Business Images/Shutterstock.com; p. 9 sashahaltam/Shutterstock.com; p. 10 Jakub Krechowicz/Shutterstock.com; p. 11 Catalin Petolea/Shutterstock.com; p. 13 karelnoppe/Shutterstock.com; pp. 17, 21 Blend Images/ Shutterstock.com; p. 18 Goodluz/Shutterstock.com; p. 19 auremar/Shutterstock.com; p. 22 Pressmaster/Shutterstock.com; p. 23 cristovao/Shutterstock.com; p. 26 B Calkins/ Shutterstock.com; p. 27 Karramba Production/Shutterstock.com; p. 29 Dmytro Vietrov/Getty Images; p. 30 Africa Studio/Shutterstock.com.

Library of Congress Cataloging-in-Publication Data

Gosman, Gillian.
Publish it: sharing your writing online / by Gillian Gosman.
p. cm. — (Core skills)
Includes index.
ISBN 978-1-4777-7390-1 (pbk.)
ISBN 978-1-4777-7391-8 (6-pack)
ISBN 978-1-4777-7389-5 (library binding)
1. Online authorship — Juvenile literature. I. Gosman, Gillian. II. Title.
PN171.O55 G67 2015
808—d23

Manufactured in the United States of America

CPSIA Compliance Information: Batch #CW15PK: For Further Information contact Rosen Publishing, New York, New York at 1-800-237-9932

CONTENTS

WRITING FOR AN AUDIENCE

Do you like to write? Some people enjoy writing in private journals or diaries. Some people write poems for their friends or family. And some people write only for assignments they're given in school. But other people want to share their writing with a wider audience, or group of viewers.

The Internet has made writing, sharing work, and connecting with readers easier than ever before. Whether you're writing an essay for school or a story for your own pleasure, you can find inspiration online. You can also plan, write, and share your work with friends both in your school and around the world. You can even be published online!

The Internet gives you the tools you need to create and share writing with an audience. In this book, we'll explore some of these digital tools.

QUICK TIP

What does it mean to be published? Some people consider it to mean that your work is included in a professional print or digital publication, such as a magazine, newspaper, or book. Other people also consider posting and sharing finished work online in **blogs** and personal websites to be a kind of publishing.

What kind of audience would you like to share your writing with? Maybe your audience includes friends and family, or maybe you want to share with a wider community of readers.

NONFICTION WRITING

You can share different kinds of writing online. Fiction is creative writing based on imagination. Nonfiction is based on real facts and events.

Two forms of nonfiction writing are expository and persuasive writing. Expository writing is any writing that tries to explain or describe something for its readers. You might see expository writing in newspapers, textbooks, and nonfiction books. You'll be expected to write expository texts in school. You may be asked to write an essay describing your favorite historical figure or a place you've visited. You may be asked to **research** a subject and explain some element of it.

QUICK TIP

In expository writing, you may structure your information as a description, comparison and contrast, or in **chronological** order. Persuasive writing is usually structured to include a claim—or argument—followed by at least three reasons. Each reason should be supported by **evidence**.

In persuasive writing, the author tries to **persuade** readers. Persuasive authors try to build a strong argument in favor of one side of an issue.

*Persuasive writing is seen in many **blogs**, articles, and* ***forums*** *where people can express their opinions. A writer might write a blog post on how they feel about women's rights and why they feel that way. They'd try to persuade others to be in favor of their argument.*

CREATIVE WRITING

Creative writing focuses on personal expression rather than sharing information with or persuading readers. Creative writers focus on the craft of writing, whether it's creating a great character in a short story or finding the perfect rhyme in a poem.

There are many genres, or kinds, of creative writing. Novels, short stories, poems, and plays are the most common kinds you'll come across. Novels, short stories, and plays introduce readers to characters, settings, and plot. Poems describe a thing, place, or feeling.

Many people consider biographies, historical accounts, and articles to be creative writing, too, as long as they're told in interesting and creative ways. All these genres share a focus on language, point of view, and theme.

QUICK TIP

Want to create a piece of creative writing, but not quite sure where to start? There are many websites that offer advice, story starters, prewriting activities, and inspiration boards to get you started.

Creative writing often explores universal human experiences, feelings, and concerns. When you write a creative piece, you're showing readers the world the way you see it.

WHAT ARE DIGITAL WRITING TOOLS?

Digital writing tools are online resources for each step of the writing process. They help you plan, compose, edit, and share your writing with a larger audience. Many websites are **interactive**.

Tools for planning come in many forms. You can find writing prompts, which are questions to kick-start your writing project. A writing prompt might be a question, an image, or a famous quotation. You can respond to a prompt by making an outline, word map, or other brainstorming tool. Or you can just start writing!

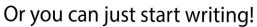

QUICK TIP

You'll find different digital tools for every genre of writing. There are digital lists of rhyming words you can use to write poetry. **Bibliography** creators help cite, or give credit, to sources in research papers. Some programs can guide you through the elements of a story. Whatever you want to write, there's an online program to help!

Next, you'll compose your written work. You can use a word processing program, such as Microsoft Word, to write and edit, or revise. There are also special digital tools for revising. Some programs check for grammar and spelling, while others check for **plagiarism**.

An example of a writing prompt for poetry might be "Write a poem about your favorite place." An example of a writing prompt for a story might be "Write a story about a talking horse." Writing prompts can be fun and helpful!

COLLABORATING WITH OTHER WRITERS

Your writing process may be very private. Maybe you like to do all your writing and editing alone. But the Internet makes it possible for writers to collaborate, or work together, at every stage of the writing process. Getting help, advice, and **criticism** from other writers can make your writing stronger.

Collaborating with other writers is easy using online drives and clouds. Information clouds are online spaces for creating, sharing, and storing information. Many clouds offer free accounts with a limited amount of storage. Dropbox (dropbox.com) and OneDrive (onedrive.live.com) are clouds writers commonly use. Simply create an account, upload your work, and invite others to view and edit it.

Some clouds, such as Google Drive (drive.google.com), allow two writers to work on a document at the same time from different computers.

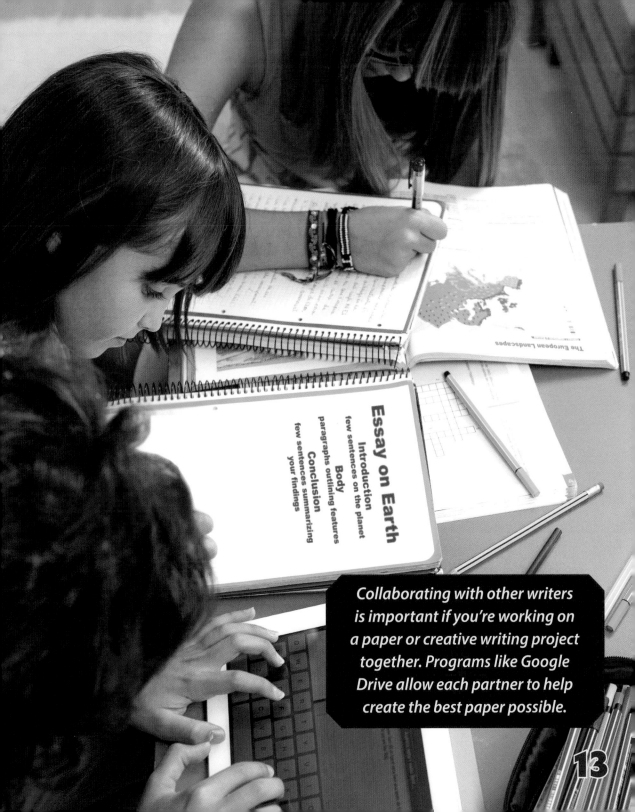

Essay on Earth

Introduction
few sentences on the planet

Body
paragraphs outlining features

Conclusion
few sentences summarizing
your findings

The European Landscapes

Collaborating with other writers is important if you're working on a paper or creative writing project together. Programs like Google Drive allow each partner to help create the best paper possible.

SOCIAL NETWORKS AND FORUMS

You can share your writing with your network, or web of friends and family, through social networking websites, such as Facebook (facebook.com) and Tumblr (tumblr.com). Public forums for writers include The Writer's Beat (writersbeat.com) and the forum at Writer's Digest (writersdigest.com). These sites are built around the idea of online conversations between writers. Users comment on shared content and experiences, and sometimes contribute their own writing.

Social networking websites aren't **designed** for publishing work, but they do offer an outlet to share your work with people you know. These websites aren't designed for making revisions, either, but they allow you to get feedback from your audience, which can help you when revising. Know that your writing may receive criticism as well as praise.

Writing forums and social networks sometimes include boards focused on inspiration, planning, mechanics, and publication. It's like having a group of writers and fans behind you during every step of the writing process!

STARTING A BLOG

A blog is a personal website made of entries, or posts. The term "blog" is a shortened version of the phrase "web log." Authors use blogs to record daily events and observations.

Blog posts are presented in reverse chronological order, which means viewers see the most recent entries first. As with social networking sites, blogs allow readers to leave comments. These comments can be good feedback for a writer to improve their writing.

You can create a blog, too! If you like writing expository pieces, you could make a blog describing all the places you've traveled. If you're a creative writer, you might post poetry or short stories on a blog. Popular blog platforms include LiveJournal (livejournal.com), WordPress (wordpress.org), and Typepad (typepad.com).

There are millions of public blogs on the Internet today. Most bloggers love the opportunity to express themselves to a worldwide audience and receive feedback from readers.

ONLINE WRITING JOURNALS

Many writers find it helpful to create a writing schedule. That usually means setting aside time every day to write. You might use this time to work on a formal piece of informational or creative writing, or you may use this time to find inspiration, brainstorm, or freewrite. When you freewrite, you write whatever comes to your mind, continuously, for a certain amount of time. Don't check for mistakes or edit—just write!

QUICK TIP

Free online writing journals include Penzu (penzu.com), Penmia (penmia.com), and 750 words (750words.com). Penzu and Penmia give you space to write notes, journal entries, and stories. 750 words encourages freewriting by providing daily prompts.

Freewriting is great practice and can help you come up with new ideas or get started on a writing project. You can start freewriting with a simple prompt, such as "Imagine you discover buried treasure in your backyard."

There are many ways to create and keep your personal writing online without sharing it with others. You can use an online journal to do daily writing exercises or keep a record of your life. Online writing journals are password protected and can be used on any web-enabled device, from your computer to your cell phone.

YOUR FINISHED WORK

You may have written a rough draft, then asked your friends, classmates, or writing community for feedback. You may have revised so many times that you feel there's nothing left to fix. Now, you may want to show others your finished product.

Some online collections for young people's writing include Figment (figment.com), Merlyn's Pen (merlynspen.org), and Teen Ink (teenink.com). Such websites allow young people to submit or post their writing and explore newly published writing from other young adults. They may host forums, educational resources, and libraries. They sometimes have contests to find the best new writing.

Literary magazines showcase new literature. *Stone Soup* (stonesoup.com) is a popular literary magazine for teens and young adults. It allows young people to submit writing online for their print magazine.

Earth Essay

Layla Johnson

When submitting your finished work to literary websites and magazines, make sure to read their submission guidelines. They may want only a certain number of pages, or they may want only writing in a certain genre or on a certain theme.

LITERARY MAGAZINES AND NEWSPAPERS

Many schools print literary magazines and newspapers that showcase student writing and visual arts. Sometimes it costs too much for a school to print these publications. Luckily, in the age of the Internet, there's another way to publish student work. Online digital publishers can take a collection of student writing and transform it into an online literary magazine or newspaper. Some digital publishers are free.

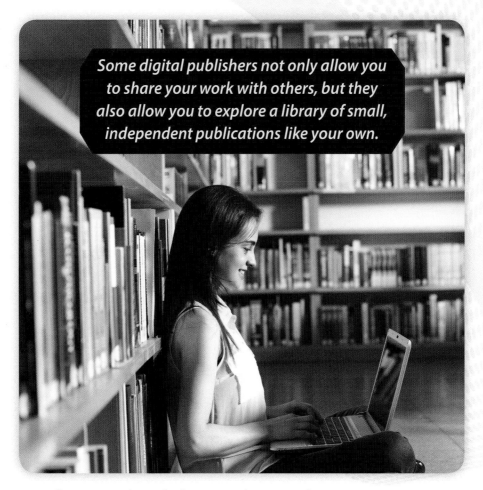

Some digital publishers not only allow you to share your work with others, but they also allow you to explore a library of small, independent publications like your own.

If your school doesn't have a literary magazine, you can make one! Find a group of readers and editors for the magazine. Collect writing from your classmates, including poetry, short stories, and articles. Then, find an online publication platform that works for you, such as Yudu (free.yudu.com) and Issuu (issuu.com). Upload your work, format it in the publication program, and share it with your school!

CLASSROOM WEBSITES

Some teachers create websites and use them as part of the classroom experience. Popular classroom website platforms include Weebly for Education (education.weebly.com), Class Jump (classjump.com), Yola (yola.com), and Glogster (edu.gloster.com). Several blogging platforms also offer education-specific blog sites, such as Edublogs (edublogs.org) from Wordpress.

When a teacher asks you to contribute your writing to a classroom website, be sure you know the expectations of the assignment and the limitations of the site. Some sites will only allow posts or comments of a certain length. Some require a password-protected login to submit content.

When sharing and commenting on student work, especially students you know and see daily, be sure to be a kind, constructive critic. Remember that everyone's writing is a work in progress!

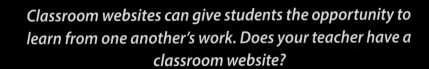
Classroom websites can give students the opportunity to learn from one another's work. Does your teacher have a classroom website?

QUICK TIP

Constructive criticism means identifying and praising a writer's strengths before making thoughtful suggestions for improvement. You might structure your comment by identifying what works in the piece of writing and then what could be revised and improved.

25

MAKING IT POP!

It's easy to publish your work on the Internet. This means that there's a lot of writing available. It's easy to get lost in the sea of writers. If you would like to attract readers and benefit from their feedback, you need to make your writing stand out. Here are a few tips.

Take the time to revise and edit. With time and hard work, you can transform a rough draft into a more polished piece of writing. Sloppy language, spelling errors, and irregular fonts will distract your readers and possibly stop them from reading. Before you submit writing, ask yourself, "Is this neat, clean, and easy to read?"

Try something new. You may love a popular writer's language, theme, or style. But chances are, many people are trying to copy that style, too. Instead, break new ground. Rather than model your characters, plots, and writing style on a favorite author, try to create your own style. Write what you know. Use your creativity and imagination to express yourself. Make your writing pop by just being you!

QUICK TIP

Creating a story based on another author's work is called fan fiction. You may use that author's characters or settings. There are many fan fiction websites for authors who like making up stories based on J.K. Rowling's *Harry Potter* series. If you write fan fiction, try to make it as inventive as possible and always give credit to the original author.

STAYING SAFE ONLINE

As we've seen, the Internet is a great place to be a writer. But it's not always a safe place for a young person. There are a few key ways to keep yourself safe.

First, never give private information. Never publish your home address, phone number, or the name of your school. Never agree to meet someone in person if you only know them online. If someone asks you to do this, tell an adult.

Don't share your usernames and passwords with anyone except a parent or teacher. When possible, adjust the privacy settings on your account so only friends, family, classmates, or a trusted audience can see your writing. When using social networks or online platforms, be on the lookout for **cyberbullying**.

QUICK TIP

Remember what you post on the Internet stays on the Internet. Before you post any content online, ask yourself if it is kind and appropriate. Is it something you will be proud of for years to come? Never post something when you're angry or upset.

Some cyberbullies insult other people's writing and try to embarrass them. On social networks, cyberbullies might send hurtful comments to someone, spread lies, post embarrassing pictures of them, or create false profiles to trick others. Report cyberbullying when you see it!

LET'S GET WRITING!

Writers have countless tools at their fingertips. The Internet offers resources for finding inspiration, planning, composing, revising, sharing, and receiving feedback. These tools allow you to connect with your friends, classmates, and young people around the world. The opportunities are unlimited, so go for it!

You might like to do creative writing for yourself or submit assignments for school. But if you want to be published, an online platform might be a great start to your writing career. Maybe someday your work will make it into print publications, such as books and literary magazines.

If you want to be a published writer, the time is now. Sit down and commit to your craft. It won't be easy, but it'll be worth it when your readers are asking for more!

GLOSSARY

bibliography (bih-blee-AH-gruh-fee) A list of the sources used or quoted in a piece of writing.

blog (BLAWG) A personal website on which someone writes about their thoughts and opinions.

chronological (krah-nuh-LAH-jih-kuhl) Based on time order.

criticism (KRIH-tuh-sih-zuhm) The judgment of both the good and bad qualities of a work of art or literature.

cyberbullying (SY-buhr-buh-lee-ihng) Bullying that happens over the Internet or text messaging.

design (dih-ZYN) To plan the way something will look or work.

evidence (EH-vuh-duhns) Facts that prove something.

forum (FOHR-uhm) An online message board where people share their opinions on a topic.

interactive (ihn-tuhr-AAK-tihv) Able to respond to a user's input.

persuade (puhr-SWAYD) To sway someone to act or think a certain way.

plagiarism (PLAY-juh-rih-zuhm) The act of passing off someone else's work as your own.

research (REE-suhrch) To study something carefully to find out more about it.

INDEX

WEBSITES

Due to the changing nature of Internet links, PowerKids Press has developed an online list of websites related to the subject of this book. This site is updated regularly. Please use this link to access the list: www.powerkidslinks.com/cosk/pub